MW01593182

REFLECTIONS

FROM THE

WORKPLACE

REFLECTIONS FROM THE WORKPLACE

 A collection of Thoughts Unspoken

Rex P. Gatto, Ph.D

GTA Press
Pittsburgh

Copyright 1995 Rex P. Gatto, Ph.D., NCC

Not to be reproduced ordistributed in any form
without the written permission of the author

ISBN 0-945997-28-0

Library of Congress Catalog Card Number 95-94476

Editor: Tony DelPrete
Book design: Jan Leo
Cover photo: Tom Bell
Cover design: Frank Lehner

Dedication

To my son, Shawn, and daughter, Maura, who will soon be in search of their destiny.

And all the people who had workshops with me causing the rethinking of my ideas about the workplace and the people in it.

The learning process is life-long for those who choose to play.

Introduction

This book of reflections was written to share the insights and feelings experienced in the workplace. We all have felt the pain, sorrow, joy and happiness of thousands of people from the workplace who have been touched by change.

The workplace, a mythical place of importance seen by many as a place of acquisition. The place where the mediocre thrive and the intellectual hide. A place striving for balance all the time driven by the bottom line.

This last decade has been filled with tremendous change and seen buzzwords come and go. "Total Quality Management", "Empowerment", "Reengineering" are all based on a common sense approach of doing what is right and appropriate, permitting people to make decisions they should make.

We need to relearn, to trust, change and grow from the experience of uncertainty. Begin to shape our talents and gifts to the changing work environment. The myths of loyalty, hard work and honesty are being questioned through mergers, cost-cutting measures and realignment of the American workforce.

Much that happens is out of our control. Part of the learning of the 90s is that we have to let go of control. The 90s are a preparation for the 21st Century. This book is based on the struggles and joys of people that we all have seen in the workplace.

Our approach to meet these cyclical demands and challenges is the ability to adapt, like a chameleon changing to the situations.

We must have the confidence within ourselves to endure, persevere and search for an inner peace and tranquility. What we look for we will find.

We don't walk alone. We are among many. The majority who feel what we feel go to work every day and produce.

We can't permit competition alone to change our thinking. We have to move to a bigger picture of helping one another, rewording what we want to become.

Calm needs to permeate and permit us on many levels to think through a self-development process providing support for each other and collectively come together. If our corporate, governmental and religious leaders don't provide inclusive leadership, then it becomes our challenge to solve the problems.

If we stop to ask the right questions, we will begin our search toward the guided discovery of the practical truth.

The challenge is ours.

Preface

Tumultuous, Changing Times

In tumultuous times we need to contemplate and adjust our inner thoughts. Those inner thoughts that drive our actions, emotions, physical and spiritual well being.

We live in a new age with science and anger balancing the scales of blind justice.

Our society is formed from generations from the hot wars of the forties, cold wars of the fifties, the killings and rebellions of the sixties, wildness and disregard of the seventies, the rhetoric of the eighties, the bombings and wars of the nineties.

A sense of deprivation exists along with this preparation time for a new century filled with change. Change abounds our inner thoughts. As individuals coming together in society, there is a need for solidarity versus the exclusive leveled societies of knowing what is right.

We need to teach ourselves to ask reflective questions rather than giving conceited answers. As our forefathers farmed and hunted for existence we require intellectually farming of new mental territory and hunting for the future.

Contemplation of self-responsibilities and accountability are necessary for clearing the way for the future. We are caretakers. We don't own it, but merely are caretakers for the next generation. The silent majority is beginning to arise and be heard addressing the loud and changing cries of the few.

The irrational thoughts of the loud are being challenged with truth. Truth and values are being reborn from an embryonic stage.

This place is being rebuilt so the arts, business, science and ideals may co-exist.

If hard questions are asked, commitment and perseverance will answer.

Contents

Career 3

The Train 4

Who Are We Now? 7

Reflections of a Friend 9

Success 11

Ode to a Coworker 17

An Older Soul 21

There Are Lots of Good People 23

I've Been Rightsized 25

Good-Bye, Dear Colleagues 28

Leader 31

Secretaries 34

Union Man 40

Legacy of Forty Years of Toil 42

The Torch Has Passed 45

Multiple Service Provider 48

Certain Uncertainty 50

Meetings 52

Years of Service 54

Time 55

The Merger 57

Caretaker 59

Pity the Pompous 62

Communication 65

First Presentation 66

The Interview 68

The Performance Appraisal Blues 71

Loyalty 73

Tomorrow's Another Day 74

Reflections 75

Total Quality in Action 78

Buzzwords 79

Becoming Angry 81

They've Come and Gone 83

Sunday 85

REFLECTIONS
FROM THE
WORKPLACE

CAREER

So I went to work because I was supposed to
It was my time to say something new
I had something to say—to be the best
The person to change the world
The person to help discover something to
    help people

So I began to say something new
But every suggestion wouldn't work, or it
    cost too much
It couldn't be done now
Yes, but . . .

The excitement inside changed to frustration
    and quit having to be said
And the ideas stopped pushing out
I looked at the clock and days went by
One less day, one less day
And we call it a career.

Reflection:
    Let the energy flow from within, rather than
    out. The inner thought will be found.

THE TRAIN

I boarded the train in the forties
A time filled with happiness and power
The war was won and factories boomed
The people were proud and the air was sweet
    with the smell of work

The train moved
And the next conflict came
A time to set boundaries in a parallel way

The train pulled in for a stop
And a war hero was found to lead us astray
He declared it important to beat the Russians
    in space
It is not art, but science that will guide our
    destination
And the train moved on

We were happy and young
Filled with Camelot
And the time to express was here
The movements were many and cries filled the
    air
With the Kennedys, King and X
And more with no names

The train slowed to view the tragedies of
    change
And the few who were happy led us astray

Even though the train went too fast
And the conductor fell
Don't worry
The track was solid and wouldn't fail
Onward to new heights

The train pulled away
As it moved ahead
It went on new track
The old was disarrayed
The train chugged south
And went high and low
By another who vowed it wasn't so

The engineer was new
But spoke with a drawl
But was honest
And something was right

The conductor called
But what about common sense?
And the future of all

The train had to slow
As the track was repaired
But what about tomorrow?
All aboard!

The track seemed to change
Or was it the view?
It all seemed to move too fast

People fell off
But the train wouldn't stop
It moved faster each day
Without even one stop

The train is well fueled
And the gears greased and oiled
Who's driving the train?
If we are all in the back

It's curious to think
The train cannot stop
Who is next
To engineer the train
The one persuading the
Public with answers

Reflection:
  Politicians come and go with glib tongues.
  The media is a powerful force, but we've
  been cheated by the loss of courageous
  people. Do you wonder what would have
  happened if the Kennedys, King and X
  would have lived?

WHO ARE WE NOW?

I went to work wanting to touch someone
Someone I hadn't known
Someone I knew I would meet

I struggled to meet the person inside
To show and bring out my thoughts
But I didn't have time

We had to get this done before three
And that had to be done by Thursday
And the boss needed this right now
And I practiced politics to get ahead

And all the while I wanted to touch someone
I continued to climb as the years went by
And worked harder to get it done
And I practiced politics to get ahead

And I continued to climb
I made decisions that made money from the
    efforts of others
I treated people carefully so they worked for
    me and I climbed

I wanted to touch someone
But he was harder to find
My career became more important

And the final promotion came
and I didn't have time to accept
I thought I had done what I was supposed to do
But I never touched that person inside

I knew I was supposed to touch someone
We were sent to do something like that

But I didn't have time
And I left too soon

Don't make a mistake
Of wanting to climb
Without understanding why

Reflection:
Remember when you entered the job market
so excited and full of life. Aging is the process
of slowly losing what it takes while being able
to afford it.

REFLECTIONS OF A FRIEND

There was a time and a place
When I saw you write
A time when I felt your presence
A time when what you said was heard

Now you have left behind the remembrances
Of what you had offered
But you live through teaching
The words of thought
The expressions of encouragement
That live in hundreds of people you encoun-
    tered

Funny
But it seems the best we do
Is give others the ability to be better
Because they have met us
Touched what we said

Many have come without thoughts of others
And the sad expression of life befalls them
The tragedy is that we don't try to touch others
Being better after than before we met

So, Sweet Prince, we part
Or do we?
We leave physically
Yet the mind's reflection to think deeper
    thoughts
Expresses ourselves in other ways
More deeply appreciate who and what
Because we were once encouraged

Maybe the best we do is help ourselves
While helping others to achieve
Achieve the unknown
Or the yet not thought

Maybe caring, respect, love are more than that
Abstracts that people discuss
But sometimes afraid to use

The questions of life
Sometimes are answered after we leave
What an irony
The hustle of life to acquire
But the fulfillment comes after we leave
The hard work
And hours of pain
Are only fulfilled when we leave

Yet another takes up the challenge
To climb the mountain
And cross the sweet fields of life
Filled with the trails and excitement of life

Maybe the best we are
Is more than now

Dedicated to John Morgan.

Reflection:
    Spirited kidders, full of life; many people
    touch and enhance our lives in the workplace.

SUCCESS

The best are rewarded
There is something different about that mortal

He listens and looks you straight in the eye
She wants to hear your point of view
First before she shares her thought

That makes you feel important
That someone listens first
What a difference I feel
When someone listens
And lets you know they heard

His voice is kind not telling
In nature—he questions to find out
Not looking at his watch

As though he cares
And doesn't have something
More important to do

She focuses the thoughts
To an end result
Work with the end
In mind she proclaims

To achieve your goal
You need to know where you're headed

He doesn't need a gimmick or two
No total quality management
Or empowerment for you
The buzzword-of-the-month club manager
He is not

She uses the views of a thousand years of
     thought
Kindness and compassion and service
Oh there's something new
She does what she says and it is simple
Listen-guide-question
With a caring approach
She uses the Bible
Not a stroke or a threat

He can change one's mind
With an empathic approach
It is his questioning style
That leads you on

Her face is receptive
With an open look
Not a hurry in mind
She takes a gentler approach

As though everyone does
She looks surprised at her own success
As people are receptive
And gives support

His boss says he's too easy
The approach that he takes
His performance evaluations are too high
Too much money the company will pay

But it is his way
To move his people
To be kind and listen
And focus the goal

She is moving up the ladder
So she is told

Why?
Because she is different than the others
Not a person of appeasement

He wants you to feel important
That's why he listens first

The company states all the things he does
But they are only buzzwords
That people want to hear

We are living in fast times
And must move ahead
Beat the clock
Or you'll be dead

It's refreshing to see someone kind in spirit
Who takes time to listen
With a smile

To move ahead
You must be fast
And quick
Playing CYA
And duck your head
Without courage but full of cunning

This woman is different
She doesn't practice politics
She practices hope

He's like an island of safety
A place
Where you can stand

She is a beam of light
And he refreshing air

He is the driver of the bus
With a clear destination
He is liked and revered
And fills others with hope

She should be president
But she can't move ahead
The system blocked her way

You wonder why he stays
Is he feeling a need
Perhaps he needs something else from us
Than what he receives

Work toward your goal
With service and might
Take time you know
What is right

Not stopping to check success is our greatest
    failure
See what you have done right
In spreading hope

He has strong followers
Who can see something inside
It's the feeling of kindness
Caring and pride

She does make a difference
And her reward is the gift of words
Kindness of thought
And gentle in nature

He is a giver of hope
The Father of joy
So what can we do to support him
In kind after all
This executive is in disguise

The rules that he follows
Came from the philosophers
Not a charlatan with a smile
Whose words are empty
With the buzzwords of today

She is searching for meaning
To challenge her life
She questions the system
Advocates for right
Stands up for conviction
And follows her word

I am better for knowing a person like this
He has touched my soul
And she opened my eyes
She treats people, not positions
With gentleness and care
I feel as though tomorrow will be a better day
Because of him, because of her
I'll return to climb the ladder
And cross the bridge

Reflection:
   Men and women who care greatly affect us;
   even if they are from different plants.

ODE TO A COWORKER

I worked with her for years
But never knew the person

I knew what she did
Don't know her inner thoughts
What were her dreams
And what made her happy
What she did outside of her job

We only talked of work
And deadlines and such
I wonder what she did
To ease her pain
From the long hours we spent
Doing the work

I knew her by position
As though she were an athlete
With a number on her back

Don't know about her children
Although I knew their names
Her husband worked hard
I saw him once or twice

It seems there is a cycle we know—
To school, then marry
And children come along
Then work to provide for our children's sake

Put your time in
Thirty years it will never end
Then just in a blink
Are we to start again

She was ready to retire
I thought I knew her well
But I really knew her by position
Rather than her goodwill

Do we make a difference each day
We all walk on the beach
Making footprints in the sand
But the waves roll in
And wipe them all away

I felt better, because over coffee
We spent time in small talk
But it seems I never knew her as a person
Just really a position

O God, what am I
No one knows my inner feelings
My deepest despair
Maybe I feel what I feel
Because it's a reflection of me
Who knows me as a person
I'm more than just a position

What can I do to know the person
With whom I work
I only know positions
That come through the door

Maybe the lesson to learn is we are people
To know—not numbers in a file
How impersonal this has all become
We must give Sunday its due
Maybe that's the problem
We haven't spread the Word

We aren't just numbers
There is a person inside
Who is more than degrees
And what we have heard
There is a need inside
That is starving for thought and recognition

I always thought there is more than this
But it's only what we think

It seems simple to change
And to be happy
But it's easier to complain to each other
The time seems to pass

But how does that help
To know the person we see

I'll remember her as I have during coffee
With a thought and a cheer

Reflection:
Sometimes the workplace seems so
impersonal. The person is only a position.
Too bad we aren't paid like athletes!

AN OLDER SOUL

This is what I want them to say
When I die
He tried
He was a gentle man among many

Stop the press
He has laid down his pen
He worked to help
Even though some resisted

Did he make a difference
He always questioned
He was quick to temper
From frustrations inside

It was a sign of the times
He pushed and struggled
But never quit

He was a modern man
With old ideals
He was straight as an arrow
With a heart that melted

He showed them strength
But was a kindred spirit
The inside was covered
With a shell of despair

That's why he sometimes would cry
The depths of his soul were challenged
Each day not by work
But the pain of others was his cross to bear

When does it stop
This world is going too fast
The merry-go-round spinning

Each of his ideals slowly perished
It's a new day of challenge
Can't you hear the conductor call
Wait! Wait for me

But the train pulled away
It was the first time he missed it
His day had passed

Stop the clock
And mark the time
You can hear the bugler's taps

Mark the tombstone carefully indeed
He came and tried and never quit
His death is physical
But his spirit lives on

In a smile and a joke and brilliant thought
From hard-working people
He is there

> Reflection:
> When someone wants to develop a career
> plan, write a retirement speech and an epi-
> taph. This helps people work backwards to
> the present, identifying what they need to
> do today.

THERE ARE LOTS OF GOOD PEOPLE

Listen to the news
Our message is clear

A lot of good people
Are working hard and steady

Don't miss what we do
We are silent, but strong

We're here, just look
We keep on producing
Missing hardly a beat

You think someone would see
We're just in front

Don't give me the news
It's not all bad and corrupt

We're right here
Hands open
To do today's duty

We continue to serve
To make a difference
But that doesn't make the papers

We've been rightsized
And angered
But we're still all around

Just take a hard look
And what do you find
We're right here in front
Supporting the way

Reflection:
Work and production are ongoing
commodities that very often go unnoticed,
yet people keep on doing something. But
what drives that inner need?

I'VE BEEN RIGHTSIZED

I tried so hard to do what was right
Frustration is building
So where do I turn
The anger is overwhelming
And I feel all consumed
Please, God, won't anyone listen to me

I've waited and worked
So loyalty would bear
A change in my life
To fulfill my ambition

I've been slapped in the face
For the last time with despair
You'll get yours
If only in my dreams

But I've worked too hard
For it to end like this

Cleaned out my desk
And walked to the door
I am so angry I could spit
Don't look me in the eye
I've had enough of this lie

I've read about violence
But what should I do
Go home with my box
And tell them what's new

You may have my job
But never my mind

Please, God, just today
I need your strength
I am consumed with fear
Will the sun come up tomorrow
I need some stability to see me through

God, will you be there
If I choose to jump?
Just need time to settle
It will take more than this

So maybe I am laid off
But not down and out
I can find a challenge elsewhere
Just give me the strength to get through

I know it's inside
I just have to find it
It's just out of reach
I know it's there deep

So where is my support
Not in a bottle
It's in my love for self and family
I'll need for comfort

My anger is still there
But time will tell
Tell it to leave
So I can again use my gifts

This is only temporary
I am not going to stop
God, just be there today
I need a little more support

Reflection:
    The rightsized person is an all too familiar
    sight. The pain of losing a job is an insur-
    mountable, stomach wrenching experience
    that makes some bitter and others stronger.
    We had a term for this in the army.

GOOD-BYE, DEAR COLLEAGUES

Do you feel the pain
Looking into my eyes
The pain and anguish
Of years of service provided
In the hope of job security

A job for life is no longer
The objective
It's a time
A place
A point of landing
But not a place of comfort

The comfort and stability are gone
With the loyalty and pride
We can't take for granted
An employment for life
Today a job is a status symbol

I am another victim of the myths
Get good grades and you'll find a good job
Work hard to get ahead
Sacrifice now to have a good future
Be loyal and you'll get promoted
Speak your mind and people will respect you

And so it goes
There must be something else
I feel like a ship passing through life
If I could only stop and stay awhile

The devastation is all around
It's like a battlefield from the Civil War
But no one realizes
That pain today is the same

At least there were parades after the war
Today you put on your face and walk the
    streets

The street is an equalizer
No one knows your importance
Just a sea of people walking
To and fro

In 1864 there were signs of warfare
For everyone to see
Bodies on the battlefield
But when I walk down the street
No one knows I've been a victim of a cutback
I don't have scars and ripped clothing
But my insides are shattered and torn

Should I continue
Or take a quick end
I'll never quit

I'll alter my shape
Like an amoeba
After all
It's just a game

If I have to learn
Let me do it in peace
For time heals all

> Reflection:
> We are slowly realizing that proverbs such
> as work hard to get ahead are myths. The
> workplace is a battlefield from which there
> are no survivors or decorated soldiers.

LEADER

Leaders are people
Filled with conviction
Who have sold their hearts
And more than it's worth
That's why many have positions
Without any clout

To lead means to serve
To serve out of love
To care, listen, support and uphold

To lead means to nurture
To guide and to question
To share and give counsel
With thoughts of their wisdom

Wisdom is using your knowledge
With loving care
To support those who follow with justice and
    right

So where have the leaders gone
We are looking around
They seem to have vanished

Most practicing politics
They've slowly slipped away

It was pride, prejudice and carelessness
That led them astray

Give me money and power
For all that it's worth

But stop!
Don't you realize
Followers need something to follow
Oh, that's a matter of my bonus
Just so it's not late

Let me lead to save the day
Yes, charge ahead
Wait, what is the plan
"Let's make money"
Full steam ahead

The quiet yet sensitive
Will wait for their day
It will come when the others perish
It won't be too long

Greed has caught them
In every possible way
In sports, hospitals
And even the zoo

Move faster and crumble
So the quiet will arise

Your tools total quality
Empowerment too
Are meaningless
Dinosaurs like you

Our day is coming
'til then, fond adieu!

Reflection:
  Leaders are servers who develop themselves
  and followers, knowing when to lead, follow,
  facilitate and listen. Pretenders of the throne
  are easier to find than cow chips in a field.

SECRETARIES

My mind is sharp
And filled with thoughts
I had to work to support myself
Didn't have time to advance through the system
To say I have a degree

But my mind is sharp
Why do they think I am not as good
I use equipment that Einstein didn't have

Each product I touch
Touch it first and touch it last
I correct the errors
And move the work
But why don't they think
My mind is sharp

My boss gets bonuses
I correct the work
Write the letter
And advance the work

But where is the thanks
Do you know what I do
I work to support the family
I bore and feed
So why don't I get the bonus I need
I advance the work
And construct the words

Why don't I advance
My mind is sharp

I don't work to be humbled
I need the money
The economy shifted
So why am I treated as someone "without"

The work I do
Is technical and new
Challenging and complex
So why do they think
My mind isn't sharp

The day is a test
To see what I can do
Rules apply to me
But where is my boss

I'll follow the light
To lead the way
It's not the job
It is the pride of a job well done

Take the time to know
My mind is full

I am the support pillar
At work and at home
My mind is sharp
And I have proven it to you

Support my family from sunset to eight
Off to work from 9 til 5
Home to relax as I pick up and deliver
And to the stove for one quick meal

Homework to bed
To start another day
Why is it I don't get paid
For this work instead

My mind is sharp
And filled with thoughts

If only they would listen
I have suggestions, but wait
Ask me first
I know the answer

Frustration seems to build
I don't know why
Maybe it's because I do it
Without a cry

To continue is madness
But why not fulfill
The fool doesn't know
The joke is on you

I am not what I do
But what I produce
The children and the work
Are the legacy I leave
At least that is honest
And filled with delight

So why do they think
My mind isn't sharp

I look in the mirror
And admire the image
The lines are from love
Not from politics and lies

Now I know the truth
It's just a game
What's important is love
Preparing the way
We don't own the right
It's only temporary

I am frustrated from thoughts of neglect
And know what I do is worthwhile
But yet

Why do they think
My mind isn't sharp

I came to the conclusion
Money doesn't mean I know less

It simply is a tool
To appease and rule
I don't fit in the system after all
I am not the work
I am who my personhood builds

I know I am somebody who delivers the goods
Seems as though my mind is intact
I don't need your review
And the person I see

I may be passive
But filled with love
My ambition is in check
But wait til I go

The peace can't run
Without a pillar of love and care
Keep your big bonus
Up in the rare air

My life is understood
And I've developed no fear

So maybe you'll find
The truth inside
When I leave
Behind the years of neglect
I'll fondly think
Of the years of appreciation
But it's time to go
I've paid my unsettled debt

> Reflection:
> Secretaries seem to be the forgotten
> workforce. They are technical producers of
> millions of documents. It is easier to replace
> a CEO than a secretary.

UNION MAN

For years I paid my dues
Thinking I would be protected
Belonged to the Brotherhood
A special place to be

The leaders negotiated
We practiced solidarity
To provide for a better life

We showed them
We held out for more

Why don't they sit down
And arm wrestle?
After all, it's just a contest
But what about me?
I am voting for change

What happened to my job?
No one said the place would close
I paid my dues
I walked the line

What will I do now
Now that I'm forty

What happened to my job?
If one more person tells us we're right
I'll practice devastation

We all held tough
Did what they said
Hey! What happened to my job?

> Reflection:
>   Unions have a time and place. But who wins
>   when the settlement of wages comes but
>   employees go?

LEGACY OF FORTY YEARS OF TOIL

It doesn't matter
Who's in office
It won't make a difference

The communication of Reagan
The good intentions of Carter
The misgivings of Nixon
The wisdom of Lincoln
It just doesn't matter

Their words have blown away
But continue we must
Many have worked
In thoughts of a better day
But something went wrong

To work and have
It's taken through
Illness by a man
I never knew

A man who wasn't born
Most of the time I toiled
A man who missed the diagnosis
And still made more money
Than I did in the first ten years of working

To work and see it all
Go, my legacy of forty years

I feel robbed by Jesse James
But Jesse had more honor
He looked you square in the eye
As he took your money

Why are all these people around my bed
I thought it was care
But came to realize I am billable

What have we come to
How much faster can we make it
How much more can they charge

So who is next
Step right up
Tell me your plan to change the world

You plan to let me keep my legacy
Hope for a better tomorrow
Your plan to change
Taxes, abortion, murder and rape
Your plan for power
Is understood

But what of my legacy
I worked and toiled for forty years
With nothing to show
But dependency on insurance
Empty promises
And disgust

Now I am sick
And being cared for by physicians
Who practice insurance

The cart is before the horse
The horse is confused
The direction is blocked
I am filled with despair

I am accustomed
To being a victim
And your words
Are meaningless and trite

But now . . . it doesn't matter
I am holding God's hand

Reflection:
Many people work hard all their lives, not
even resting Sundays, finding themselves
tired and worn, waiting to touch the hand
of God.

THE TORCH HAS PASSED

My old professor died the other day
I read his name in the obituaries

It seemed so hard and cold
To read his name and what he did
He was so much more
He looked like a professor
With white hair and a beard

He was the man who introduced me
To the world of science and knowledge
Who argued his point with clarity
Who held his ground among colleagues

The obituary didn't mention
His values and ideas
Will live through each student
The many times we speak with authority
Somehow he speaks too

It isn't enough
To have gone to the ivory tower
With a foundation of granite
To find a mason
Who was willing to carve
Shape and polish the marble
The rough stone he had found

To say softly
You have carried on
The purpose of my mission

I need one more phrase
One more thought
One more statement of support

The torch is passed
And I accept
The words will be spoken
The ideals carried forth

In these troubled times
We'll play a game
And drink a brew

The light still shines
Smile softly
And carry that thought
The pen isn't dry
And there is so much
More to say

I'll go back to work
With a new fervor
Because there are
A pair of new shoes to fill

To remember
Your ideals and values
That we all believed
Need to be lived

I now am the old guard
Protecting the treasure
The lit torch to be passed

Dedicated to Larry Knolle

Reflection:
   Many of us are lucky to have had a person in
   our lives who quietly challenged us to be
   better, a motivator disguised as a questioner.

MULTIPLE SERVICE PROVIDER

When I got out of school
I knew what I could do
I knew it all
And was confident and sure

Slowly I realized
There was much to know
The more I learned
The more inadequate I've become

I am doing much more
Than what I practiced
No one said it was like this
When it's supposed to be that

I've come to realize
To succeed I need to offer myself
Mind, tongue and stomach

Piece by piece
Slowly I give in
This offer is more than I can bear

But if it's service you want
It's service you'll get
To continue I must
Like a burr on a wild animal
I'll travel to find another secure place
Somewhere in my mind

Reflection:
    Today we have to be multiple service
    providers rather than specialists, being
    held accountable to do what the boss can't.

CERTAIN UNCERTAINTY

I'm afraid
Don't know what to expect
I have followed the myths
Without protection

How much more can we take
Another political suggestion
A moment in time

It doesn't matter much any more
It's time to find religion
But another charlatan appears
So where do we turn
The honor of our work is gone
It's how much money you make

What happened to being a righteous person
Not a position
Seems you sit in the first pew
To be noticed
And retreat to the back
To quietly reflect

Where do we go if there's no place to turn
We have come through the worst
It is a realization of pride

Uncertainty is just a place
There is nothing to fear
It's become a blanket
And shelter from the storm
It's a challenge for new talent to secure

The game continues to be played
I'll sit this one out
Let the other players play
I already know the score

When uncertainty is a friend
We will truly know the truth
This is just the preparation
Time for the next century
Breaking the old and
Preparing the new

Reflection:
    Once we can deal with uncertainty, we will
    have learned the lesson from the
    transformational 90s.

MEETINGS

Meetings, meetings everywhere
With nothing truly gained
Another meeting
Has passed to show
The level of my rank

Meetings without truth
Trust and loyalty
Disguised as productive courses of action

To find out
What people truly think
We have to take a break
Retire to the rest rooms
Where the truth
Is momentarily spoken

"I should have . . . ."
"I'm going to tell him . . . ."
The blustering cry of the wild
Blaming, snorting
And bragging of actions
That will never be

Return to the meeting
With sobering thoughts of reality
To the meeting
Watching the clock
And fantasizing

Planning my work, working my plan
For later
What's this meeting about
No goal
Just talk

I know we did something
I've been here for hours
I feel like an elementary school child
Waiting to be dismissed

Another religious experience
The meeting is over
We are all leaving
With different agendas
Messages and thoughts

Another empowered team meeting
Quality surely is at work

Reflections:
    What is the goal?
    What was accomplished?
    What did we agree on?
    How do you feel?

YEARS OF SERVICE

I worked for minimum wage
And the thoughts of protecting my family
With benefits of medical, dental, eye care

I am proud of what I've done
Though the job is routine

A struggle that can be endured
A career that practiced following demands

Who is the fool
The managers who worry
Or me
I can sleep at night

I leave and forget
My daily pattern broken
A new mental extension begins
Tomorrow's another day

Reflection:
    Everything in life is a tradeoff; some of
    us work to live, others live to work.

TIME

Looking out from within the hourglass
I've been caught
I can feel the sand through my hands

As it is pulled through
The black hole
Of continual things to do

Projects, family, phone calls
Celebrations, holidays
All blend into one
As the sand continues to fall

Almost like a punishment
I can feel the pressures of time
The sand never stops from falling
No matter what I do

Time
Followed by time
Followed by time

The only stoppage is death
The equalizer
When the hourglass runs dry

Faster, quicker in a race
To beat the clock
An impossible dream

The sand continues to move
As I look out of my glass
Billable hours are playmates
For the professional

Relaxing, leisure and vacation
Is but time followed by the schedule
Punching the clock
What are we doing
Whatever it is
Try to do more

The sand is never ending
It continues to flow
Use your time wisely
To break your fall

This is just another day
The hourglass has caught me
But only time will tell

Reflection:
Time is elusive. The more we try to beat it
the more we lose. If faster were better,
Einstein might have failed.

THE MERGER

Who's who
And what's what
Who are these people
Down the hall

A few mistakes
And all is lost
I knew these investments
Wouldn't work

The halls are empty
There is a new smell in this place
The light seems diffused
The friendliness of the past

The first things to go
Weren't the people
It was trust and communication
Replaced by fear

I've read about this
But it's not supposed
To happen to me

Why am I left
What happened to my friends
The name is gone
And so is its personality

Like the death
Of a ailing longtime friend
Parting is bittersweet

Reflection:
    Mergers have altered the course of business,
    merging the inner thoughts of the person -
    who is left with disbelief.

CARETAKER

We are only here temporarily
Holding positions for the next generation
A generation ill prepared
Impatient
Yet filled with ambition
And strength
Just like us

We are too concerned
With providing for ourselves
And collecting bonuses and promotions
As insignificant badges of honor
Losing sight of the goal
Lacking property
Doesn't mean you are without value

Forging a kinder new frontier
A frontier of tranquility
Forth righteousness
Honor and peace

But we don't have time
Greed has replaced the goal
Not who you are
Or searching for kindred spirits
But what you do
How much you have acquired

The false esteem of the job
Provides a temporary sense of power
But when the cord is cut
We will have to justify
The actions

We are the caretakers
Forging the way
But we have lost our trail
And detoured
Toward a faster sense
Of self-gratification

What have we left
It will soon be defined
For a better tomorrow
Should be our goal

Like the loggers of the North
We have harvested our lumber
But what trees have been planted
To ensure the next load
Who is next with the ax

We are holding our place
Not as owners
But caretakers
Of what is to come

Like batters at the plate
One by one we approach
All waiting to get
Our chance at first base

Some knowing this thought
Will take three hard swings
Others hoping for four slow balls
For a walk

We are caretakers
Harvesting our bounty
Let's plant seeds
For tomorrow
The values for life
Money is fleeting
Life, is a goal

Reflection:
    Do we really hold a job and space, or are
    we caretakers for the next generation?

PITY THE POMPOUS

Did God make them that way
Filled with self-importance
Or did it just happen at work one day

They always seem to have a frown
It replicates the tone of their voice
They always know the answer

Like a wolf watching its prey
They peer through their glasses
Showing a slight misconception
Of how they take in your message

When they attend meetings
It becomes a religious experience
Honing in on insignificance
Like a fighter jet
Zeroing in on an enemy plane
Following the radar screen
To find a simple phrase
And debating it with fervor

Who cares, only the pompous
Telling you why this or that has failed
Others look at their watches
Waiting for a break in the barrage

They look for support
To get another to speak
Really only wanting agreement
To continue to fuel their attack

The meeting is over
But continue they must
For they are the pompous
With an abrasive touch

No one confronts
Just isn't worth it
Who cares
It's more fun to talk
Behind their back

The shame of it is
They have covered their soul
Afraid to have it touched by kindness

Maybe we should stop and ask
How they feel
But instead avoid them
At all cost

It would be nice
If they found a close friend
To confide
And express inner thoughts
That makes someone
Vulnerable and nice

No matter what happens
There is always someone
Changing their face
Size and shape
The pompous survive

They return
Even after they're gone
There is always one
To carry on

No wonder work is slow
It's either listening or talking
Awaiting the storm

It's more pleasant
When they're gone
We will wait the day
Too bad they're so pompous
They may have something
Good to say

But it's lost in the sadness of arrogance
Beyond which there may be hope
But the pompous are back again
Quick, run for cover

> Reflection:
> Why do some people look for insignificant
> points, making them significant, nit-picking
> their way to the top? Their abrasiveness is
> second only to the time they waste.

COMMUNICATION

Communication
The key to success
And the cause of all conflict

The reason for love
And the provoker of war

The declaration of truce
And the enemy's call

The reason for frustration
And the prayer for us all

> Reflection:
> Communication is like the cardiovascular
> system: if it gets blocked it can cause death.

FIRST PRESENTATION

I know it's coming
That dreaded day
But let's make it fun
In spite of the pay

The topic was given
The research compiled
My boss and friends
Will be readily filled

So with the confidence
And fortitude I'll begin
My hands are sweating
My heart pounding through

The introduction is finished
I am ready to speak
Please someone help me
My first line is here

Who are all these people
Listening to me speak
Why did they come
Don't they realize the pain

The first words are out
This isn't so bad
I've finished the overview
Now on to the meat

I like these people
Looking at me
This may be fun
Words are flowing right out of my mouth

The clock is ticking
I have much more to say
My boss is frantically waving
I've passed my time

I want to come back
To face another crowd
Why do presentations
Seem so hard

No wonder politicians
Get such a buzz
The command, presence
The power are thrilling
Are sport

Reflection:
  Sweaty hands, dry mouth, the pounding
  heart anticipating the first presentation.
  Later, the joys of presentation and the
  laughing at ourselves.

THE INTERVIEW

The resume was prepared and mailed
The schedule set
The hour approached
And the nerves were upset

Let the games begin
With a smile and a cheer
How much should I say

They seem friendly at first
But what are their motives
I'll trust my responses
And make it the truth

I wonder what
The questioner thinks of me
What hidden, cleverly disguised
Questions will be asked

The first interviews done
Now onto the next
This place is too quiet
It just can't be

Like a house
When company comes
All neat and presentable
This place seems to me

But at home
The clothes are hidden
Under the bed
It's what they aren't saying
That frightens me
What have they hidden
Why did that last person leave

How many people
Interview well
Saying the right things
Impressing them with word
Thought and deed

Only to be an ogre
With tyrannical glee

No one admits
To hiring a jerk
But I've seen many people
That have passed the test

On to the third interview
I am moving ahead
I wonder how many applicants
Have made it this far

Repeating the same things
Over and over again
With a smile
And wonderment of anticipation

The words now come
Trippingly off the tongue
Like a broadcaster of the news
I present myself

I present my case
With fervor and enthusiasm
Yet a gentle touch of humility
I must be doing well
Please wait in the hall

I'm excited
Can't wait to go home
And tell the news

Here comes the interviewer
Step into my office
My heart is pounding
I can hardly speak
My mind is racing
What will be said
Yes! Yes!

Come back tomorrow

Reflection:
Interviewing is the lost art of putting the right person in the right job. If interviewers did a great job there would be less trouble in the workplace.

THE PERFORMANCE APPRAISAL BLUES

Nervously walking down the hall
To the room of torture and pain
The room where they practice punishment

Sitting in the chair
Where the story begins
The place of destiny
The beginning of work-related life

If only this cup would pass
The stories I've heard
The ogre is waiting
I am ready . . . knock on the door

"Come in, sit down"
Why is she smiling
"How are you doing?"
This start is friendly

I am waiting
For the torture and pain to begin
Discussing my thoughts,
Strengths and development
Sure, but when does the pain
And torture begin

I've worked hard
Just as she said
This is my first time
In the chair
It doesn't feel so bad

This was an experience
I'll live to tell
Have to think of a fish story
To carry the day

They lied
This process wasn't torture and pain
An honest appraisal
Of what I do

I'm lucky
The manager's fair
This surely was something to learn

Reflection:
    Performance appraisal should be a time of
    celebration and development, not a time to
    disburse money.

LOYALTY

Loyalty is gone
It moved away
Leaving
With the last cutback
Of people who gave their all

People who thought
I'll stay here for my career
But changes were made
And many displaced

Loyalty had been replaced
By fear, uncertainty
And people who watch the clock

The companies
Are going through metamorphosis
To meet their new challenges
What's left
A workforce redefining

Their sense of tranquility
This is our time
For transformation
Changing the face
Fidelity
Business and time

Reflection:
   Loyalty today is toward "me."

TOMORROW'S ANOTHER DAY

So what did I accomplish
Today was a bust
The phone rang off the hook
And people dropped in
To pass the time
What have I done

Maybe
I did more than I think
Giving myself credit
For the answers I provide
The input at meetings
And the papers I'll leave behind

Today, leave with pride
Accomplishing much
There is more that I did
Than having to do

Tomorrow's a new day
Challenging much

> Reflection:
>   At the end of the day focus on what you
>   did, services you provided, not a "to do"
>   list for tomorrow.

REFLECTIONS

I can't quite describe
The feelings I have
Looking at the buildings
That house thousands from 9 to 5

What goes on
In all those offices
Duplicating work
Thinking it's original
Mediocre minds
Producing the work of philosophers

The mighty
Flexing their muscle
Protecting turf
The satisfied
Talking through the day

The busy bee
Working to accomplish
The work of many
The peddler
Preparing his can for donations
During rush-hour traffic

What goes on
In all those buildings
How will humankind
Benefit from today's
Work and struggle
How will our burdens
Be lessened
And our hearts
Filled with joy

Someone up there
Maybe writing a book
To save the world
Who will listen
They are hard at work

The next cure for cancer
Maybe discovered
While the next scam
Is planned
Until it's uncovered

The rain beats against them
The sun reflects its beams
The cold winter wind blows
What happens
In those buildings
So tall and straight

The revolving door moving
Letting them in and out
Those minds
Of the future
Explaining the past

Losers, winners
The proud full of esteem
The buildings
The protectors of all
Like fortresses
For combat
Housing the many
So a few can work

Reflection:
    Did you ever look at skyscrapers and
    wonder what all the people inside do—if
    they all worked hard from nine to five we
    could take Fridays off.

TOTAL QUALITY IN ACTION

Is "total quality" the place to be
Out in front of the crowd
Diligently working
To become something new
Striving to do what is right
The first time through

Making difficult choices
And taking risks
Leaving the process authentically
Creating enhanced change
For a new day of thinking

Being a model for tomorrow
Providing a collaborative leadership
In a new direction
For all to accept

Being vulnerable
Human
Honest
Willing to chance today
For tomorrow's progress will come

Reflection:
   Total quality is the application of common
   sense.

BUZZWORDS

"Total quality"
Is the place to be
Out in front of the crowd
For everyone to see
Follow the immortal words
Of that last, profound sayer
Showing the painted face
Like the Pharaohs
Using words very appropriately
Without substance
Conviction
And honesty
Diligently exhibiting
Every tendency

"Empowerment"
Another word for thee
Stopping
To freeze a frame
In reality
Giving lip service
Of valuing others
As their decisions
Are changed in secret

Empowering others
To value their thoughts
Ideas and beliefs
Yet controlling the essence
Of what they do

CEOs playing politics
With fragile employees' egos
Appeasing to succeed

Promoting the fraudulent
Thought-thinking adults
Are children to be controlled
Guiding them like puppets
On strings

"Buzzwords"
A program for today
Gone tomorrow

Reflection:
Buzzwords create the illusion of leadership
and the mirage of vision.

BECOMING ANGRY

Each year is to be better
More humane and filled with challenge
What happened to less stress
And better working conditions

Treating adults like adults
Why does a rage build
To a point of eruption
Leaving in it's path
Destruction
People who have lost self-respect

Who is to blame
There must be
An explanation for this news

People like you and me
Lost the coping power
To continue
The unattended sick
Whose only thought
Is to lessen their pain

What are we doing
In this perfect world
Of do more with less
And cut head count
With disregard

Organizations are too big
To touch their humanness
To attend the sick
What will we do
If nothing
Come up with more rhetorical
Phrases to explain

Like balloons above
Our heads filling
With air
Anger seems to continue

Reflection:
   Supporting one another, being empathetic,
   listening first, are more people oriented skills
   than words of leadership, quality and empowerment.

THEY'VE COME AND GONE

Like fueled planes
Leaving the jet way
They line up to be heard
Speaking empty promises
On issues
That may never be

Gathering followers
With zeal and fortitude
To carry their message

The checks and balances
And rhetoric continue
And the populous
Take in the rhetoric
Like prize fighters
Ready to take a dive
Promoting half truths
With hidden agendas
Win, winning first
Gaining fame, power, fortune

Change history
And meet their destiny
They continue to come
Questioned by reporters
They live and die
On the air waves
Supporting goodwill
Towards all
With words of exclusion
And programs for the poor

They line up like
Planes waiting for combat
We listen and vote
They'll be no difference
None that we know
Their words are empty
Of love, hope and care

The faces all change
But the words flow like wine
It continues to amaze the observer
They come and go through a revolving door

I'd rather listen to music
And contemplate my fate alone

Reflection:
    A sign of the times; vote the bums out.

SUNDAY

Eleven a.m. Sunday morning
The most segregated time of the week
When many good people
Mixed with hypocrites
Practice religion

The religion of show and words
Discussing the deeds of the week
Reflecting on the actions
All for the benefit of the people

The energy of religion
Focuses on forgiveness
Strengthening the meek
And vindicating the wicked

Returning to work Monday
For another dose of power
Thus beginning
The impersonal expressions of work
Business as usual

What happens
Between Sunday and Monday morning
The altruistic expressions
Of values and beliefs
Dissipate
Floating in air

For another week
Business is money
Yet, the meek
Shall inherit the earth?

Reflection:
Religions are full of hypocrites, but the
meek and devoted lead the way.

REFLECTIONS FROM THE WORKPLACE

is Rex Gatto's fourth book exploring issues from the world of business. The reflections represent the struggles people endure from 9 to 5. This collection of thoughts represents the unique challenges of the 90s.

GTA PRESS
733 Washington Road
Pittsburgh, PA 15228
412~344~2277 (voice)
412~344~3828 (fax)